101 Gourmet ice cream CREATIONS for EVERY CRAVING

WENDY PAUL

FRONT TABLE BOOKS
SPRINGVILLE, UTAH

Text © 2012 by Wendy L. Paul
Photographs © 2012 by Marielle Hayes

ISBN: 978-1-4621-1013-1

Published by Front Table Books, an imprint of Cedar Fort, Inc., 2373 W. 700 S., Springville, UT 84663
Distributed by Cedar Fort, Inc., www.cedarfort.com

LIBRARY OF CONGRESS CATALOGING-IN-PUBLICATION DATA

Paul, Wendy, author.
101 gourmet ice cream creations / Wendy Paul.
pages cm
ISBN 978-1-4621-1013-1
1. Ice cream, ices, etc. 2. Cookbooks. I. Title.
TX795.P38 2012
641.86'2--dc23
          2012001012

Cover and page design by Angela D. Olsen
Cover design © 2012 by Lyle Mortimer
Edited by Emily S. Chambers

Printed in China

10 9 8 7 6 5 4 3 2 1

Printed on acid-free paper

Dedication

Thank you for teaching me the value of working hard and playing hard, for being my biggest supporter, a wonderful father, and for always being willing to taste test my goodies. Thank you for not being too angry when I dumped the salt water from the ice cream machine out on your lawn and killed your grass. And last but not least, thank you for being a wonderful grandpa to my children. I am the luckiest girl in the world!

Contents

We all Scream for Ice Cream!

WHAT GOES BETTER with cupcakes, cookies, and cake bites?

YOU GUESSED IT. Ice cream.

A PERFECT TREAT that will cool you down on a hot summer day—even on the coldest, wintry day, ice cream will hit the spot. It's a comfort treat that is soothing, refreshing, and satisfying. Some of my fondest childhood memories involve making—and, of course, eating—homemade ice cream.

ICE CREAM HAS BEEN an American tradition for centuries. Even Thomas Jefferson enjoyed homemade ice cream with friends after a good meal. It is a tradition that is timeless. Once you try homemade ice cream, it will be hard to purchase a half-gallon at the store. Its fresh and rich taste is captivating and rather addicting. There's nothing better than good food, good family and friends, and good traditions.

FROM COOKIES AND CREAM, to Chocolate Raspberry Trifle, Key Lime Pie, and Roasted Strawberry, inside this book there's a recipe for every craving. It always has been, and what will be, that matters: It's what's on the inside that counts. Fresh cream, fresh ingredients, pure cane sugar.

YOU CAN'T BUY HAPPINESS, but you can make ice cream. That's the same kind of thing.

ENJOY YOUR ICE CREAM JOURNEY!

—Wendy L. Paul

Tips *for* Success

ALONG THE WAY in my ice cream journey, I learned a few valuable tips. I'd like to share them with you because we all deserve to have wonderful successes making homemade ice cream.

WHEN MAKING FRUIT ICE CREAM, it's best to have a higher fat recipe. The natural water in the fruit tends to lessen the rich creams, making your ice cream less creamy and less tasty. Also, when you add the fruit to the recipe, make sure you take the time to dice and sugar your fruit, add the lemon juice, and put it in the fridge. The sugar will help lower the freezing point of the fruit, making it less icy when you freeze it; also the natural juices that come out of the fruit will help flavor your ice cream perfectly.

REFRIGERATE OR FREEZE THE GOODIES. When adding goodies and candies to your ice cream, do so in the last few minutes just before your ice cream is done. Fold in the candies or goodies just before freezing. That way, the goodies will stay mixed throughout the ice cream and not sink to the bottom. Also, for your additions, whether fruit, chocolate, or candies, refrigerate or have the goodies already frozen. This is a great tip—works every time. Follow the recipe directions, of course. You never want to add warm or hot goodies to ice cream.

EGG-BASE RECIPES VERSUS CREAM-BASE RECIPES. The eggs add a richness and texture to your ice cream. Period. If you don't want to put raw eggs in your ice cream, you can cook the eggs, cream, and sugar mixture over low heat until 160 degrees, stirring constantly, forming a custard. Remove the custard from the heat and refrigerate until cold.

Then follow the recipe's directions and process in your ice cream maker. Or you can choose from the other ice cream recipes I have in the Basics section. These egg-based ice creams will freeze better and longer than your cream-based ice creams. If you make your cream-based ice cream and then know that you are going to eat the entire batch immediately, this is no problem. I can think of worse things than this, darn it!

FREEZE AHEAD YOUR INDIVIDUAL ICE CREAM SCOOPS. This is a great tip when you are serving ice cream to a large crowd—whether for birthday parties, BBQ's, or family gatherings. It allows each premade scoop to be placed rather quickly on top of your cake, pie, cupcake, or beside your cookies or cake bites. Use a paper liner and cupcake pan, scooping one generous ice cream scoop into each liner. Repeat until all liners are filled. Place in the freezer until ready to serve. Toss your paper liners in the garbage when you are done.

EACH RECIPE IN THIS BOOK makes about one quart of ice cream. If you want less, you can reduce each recipe by half, which will make about one pint—the perfect single serving if you are my brother-in-law Mark or his father, Bob. Or if it was me, it would still be a double serving. Some larger homemade ice cream machines allow you to make more than one quart at a time. In that case, you can double the recipes in this book, but make sure you still have at least 20–30 percent airflow through your machines, or only fill your canisters ¾ full. This will ensure a thick, heavy ice cream for your end result.

HOMEMADE ICE CREAM MACHINES. There is a wide variety of ice cream machines on the market. Some range from $200–400. But don't be alarmed—I have found that you don't need a machine that is large or expensive. Some stand mixers have ice cream machine attachments, and there are some great machines for under $100. Or you can use a recipe for ice cream in a bag. You will still be able to enjoy a wonderful bowl of homemade ice cream even if you don't have an ice cream machine. But I highly recommend purchasing a nice ice cream machine, especially if you are going to be making a lot of ice cream.

MIX IT UP, HAVE FUN, AND COMBINE flavors and recipes to make your "perfect" ice cream creation.

LAST BUT NOT LEAST: anyone can make homemade ice cream.

The Basics

Rich and Creamy Vanilla

This recipe will stand the test of time. It's perfect in every way.

MAKES
1 quart

2 egg yolks

¾ cup sugar

2 cups heavy cream

1 cup 2% milk

1 tsp. pure vanilla extract

WHISK together egg yolks and ¼ cup sugar until eggs are light yellow in color and fluffy. Whisk in the rest of the sugar.

COMBINE cream, milk, and vanilla extract, and whisk together until completely combined. (If raw eggs in your ice cream makes you uncomfortable, go to pages ix-x to learn how to cook this mixture.) Then chill in your fridge until cold, best if overnight.

TRANSFER your chilled cream liquid into your ice cream machine and make according to manufacturer's directions.

Creamy Vanilla

This recipe contains less fat than Rich and Creamy Vanilla and does not have any eggs in it. Perfect for specific dietary needs, but still has the heavy, creamy texture you desire.

½–¾ cup sugar

2 cups cream

1 cup 2% milk

1 tsp. pure vanilla extract

MAKES
1 quart

WHISK together all ingredients until combined.

TRANSFER your cream liquid into your ice cream machine and make according to manufacturer's directions.

Skinny Vanilla

In this recipe, though light in the cream department, there is no compromise on taste and texture. It's simply delicious. This recipe is for my mom—she has been urging me to create a lower fat dessert. Love you, Mom!

MAKES
1 quart

½ cup sugar

2 cups light cream

I cup 2% milk

I tsp. pure vanilla extract

WHISK together all ingredients until combined.

TRANSFER your cream liquid into your ice cream machine and make according to manufacturer's directions.

Cancún Coconut

An alternative base—non-dairy and simply delicious.

2 cups coconut cream or cream of coconut
2 cups coconut milk (whole or light)
1 tsp. vanilla

WHIP your coconut cream or cream of coconut until thick.

FOLD in your coconut milk and vanilla.

TRANSFER your cream liquid into your ice cream machine
and make according to manufacturer's directions.

MAKES
1 quart

Fruity and Fabulous

Ann's Lemon
Supreme

Ann's Lemon Supreme

This was one of the very first homemade ice creams I fell in love with. The taste is out-of-this-world good.
It has the perfect combination of lemons and cream. Thanks, Ann!

1 Basic recipe of your choice (p. 2–5)

1 tsp. lemon extract

2 lemons, zested and juiced

MIX together the lemon extract and zest to your Basic recipe,
whisking until combined.

PLACE mixture in your machine and follow manufacturer's directions in freezing.
During the last 5 minutes of the freezing process, add the lemon juice.

• • • • • • • • • • • • • • • • • • •

VARIATIONS

LEMON BLUEBERRY

Add 1 cup blueberry pie filling and 1 ½ cups fresh blueberries during the mixing process.

LEMON RASPBERRY

Add 2 cups fresh or frozen raspberries and 3 tablespoons raspberry jam or preserves
during the mixing process.

MAKES
1 quart

Roasted
Strawberry

Roasted Strawberry

*For this recipe, roasting your strawberries is key. It brings out
the richness and color of the strawberries.*

1 Basic recipe of your choice (p. 2–5)
1 lb. fresh strawberries, washed and dried
4 Tbsp. balsamic vinegar
4 Tbsp. sugar

TOSS sugar and balsamic vinegar with the strawberries.

PLACE on a cookie sheet in a single layer and bake at 300 degrees for 30 minutes.

REMOVE from the oven and cool. Finely chop or blend your strawberries until smooth.

PLACE strawberries and all the juices in a sealed container in your fridge overnight
or at least 4 hours.

ADD strawberries and juice to the Basic recipe, stirring together until combined.

PLACE mixture in your machine and follow manufacturer's directions in freezing.

MAKES
1 quart

VARIATION

STRAWBERRY CHEESECAKE

Add one 8-ounce package of softened cream cheese. Then in the last five minutes,
add ½ cup crushed graham cracker crumbs.

Key Lime Pie

Key Lime Pie

Yes, of course I had to include key lime in this recipe book.
It wouldn't be complete without it. It's a keeper!

1 Basic recipe of your choice (p. 2–5)

2 limes, zested and juiced

½ cup crushed graham crackers

ADD the lime zest to your Basic recipe, whisking together until combined.

PLACE mixture in your machine and follow manufacturer's directions in freezing.

DURING the last 5 minutes of the freezing process, add the lime juice and the crushed graham crackers.

MAKES
1 quart

Banana Nut

Banana Nut

Seriously, you think you are eating banana bread while eating this ice cream.
It was one of the favorites for the taste testing. You can't just eat one bite.

1 Basic recipe of your choice (p. 2–5)

3 ripe bananas, mashed

1 ½ tsp. walnut flavoring

½ cup chopped walnuts, optional but encouraged

WHISK together your mashed bananas, walnut flavoring, walnuts, and Basic recipe until combined.

PLACE mixture in your machine and follow manufacturer's directions in freezing.

• • • • • • • • • • • • • • • • • • • •

VARIATION

HUNKY MONKEY

Fold 2 cups Chocolate Ganache (p. 88) into your ice cream just before serving, leaving chunks and swirls.

MAKES
1 quart

Triple Berry

I have found that even during the winter, I crave a fresh fruit ice cream . . . That's why I love the triple berry bag of frozen fruit you can get at most of the local grocery stores. It's convenient and pretty inexpensive—and pretty awesome.

1 Basic recipe of your choice (p. 2–5)

3 cups triple berry mixture, defrosted

4 Tbsp. sugar

1 tsp. cinnamon

IN a small sauce pan, heat berries, sugar, and cinnamon, and cook for 10–12 minutes, stirring every few minutes.

REMOVE from the stove and place berries in the fridge in a covered container.

CHILL overnight or for at least 2 hours.

COMBINE the berries with the Basic cream recipe and stir to combine.

PLACE mixture in your machine and follow manufacturer's directions in freezing.

MAKES
1 quart

Mango Lime

How could you go wrong with the combination of mangoes and limes? (P. S. I even used some dehydrated mangoes from my food storage to make this recipe, and it tasted great!)

1 Basic recipe of your choice (p. 2–5)

2 limes, zested and juiced

4 ripe mangoes, peeled and pureed into a smooth consistency

COMBINE your mangoes and lime zest with your Basic recipe.

PLACE mixture in your machine and follow manufacturer's directions in freezing.

DURING the last 5 minutes of mixing, fold in the lime juice and serve.

MAKES
1 quart

Sour Cream
Blueberry

Sour Cream Blueberry

Colorful and beautiful, this ice cream is classic.

1 Basic recipe of your choice (p. 2–5)

1 cup sour cream

2 cups blueberry pie filling

1 cup fresh blueberries

MIX sour cream, pie filling, and fresh blueberries with your Basic recipe. Stir to combine. Place mixture in your machine and follow manufacturer's directions in freezing.

● ● ● ● ● ● ● ● ● ● ● ● ● ● ● ● ● ● ●

VARIATIONS

SOUR CREAM PEACH

1 Basic recipe of your choice (p. 2–5)

1 cup sour cream

3 cups peaches, pureed

COMBINE sour cream and pureed peaches with your Basic recipe. Stir to combine.

PLACE mixture in your machine and follow manufacturer's directions in freezing.

MAKES
1 quart

SOUR CREAM RASPBERRY

1 Basic recipe of your choice (p. 2–5)

1 cup sour cream

2 cups raspberries, mashed

COMBINE sour cream and mashed raspberries with your Basic recipe. Stir to combine.

PLACE mixture in your machine and follow manufacturer's directions in freezing.

Piña Colada

Piña Colada

This ice cream is good for any celebration. It's good in a cone, in a bowl, or eaten just out of the carton or container. I would recommend starting with the Cancún Coconut Basic recipe.

1 Basic recipe of your choice (p. 2–5)

1 tsp. coconut extract

16 oz. can of crushed pineapple, with juice

COMBINE your Basic recipe with the coconut extract and pineapple and juice.

PLACE mixture in your machine and follow manufacturer's directions in freezing.

MAKES
1 quart

Coconut Cream Pie

This ice cream was in the first group of ice creams I made—the taste testing went well, and after making it again, it was even more of a hit.

1 Basic recipe of your choice (I recommend the Cancún Coconut, p. 5)

1 tsp. coconut extract

1 cup shredded coconut

½ cup crushed graham crackers

COMBINE your basic recipe with the coconut extract and shredded coconut.

PLACE mixture in your machine and follow manufacturer's directions in freezing.

DURING the last 5 minutes of mixing, fold in the graham crackers and serve.

MAKES
1 quart

Grilled Spicy Peach

I got this idea from grilling peaches and serving with a scoop of ice cream. Why not combine the flavors together in one dessert? That's how this recipe was born . . . combining flavors to make a perfect ice cream.

1 Basic recipe of your choice (p. 2–5)

6 medium peaches

2 Tbsp. olive oil

½ tsp. cinnamon

½ tsp. nutmeg

½ tsp. cloves

½ tsp. ginger

CUT the peaches in half, removing the pit.

RUB the peaches with the olive oil, and grill, skin side down first, for 3–4 minutes on medium heat. Turn the peaches over, flesh side down. Cook for another 3–4 minutes.

REMOVE the peaches from the grill and place in the fridge until the peaches are cool to the touch.

PULL the skin off and puree the peaches until smooth. Cover and refrigerate until chilled.

MIX your chilled peaches with your seasonings and Basic recipe until smooth.

PLACE mixture in your machine and follow manufacturer's directions in freezing.

MAKES
1 quart

Harvest Apple
Walnut

Harvest Apple Walnut

Fall is my favorite time of year. Not only do I love the color of the leaves, but also I love the fruits and vegetables that are in season. The flavors are amazing, especially freshly picked apples.

1 Basic recipe of your choice (p. 2–5)

2 cups apple pie filling

1 ½ tsp. walnut flavoring

½ cup roasted walnuts, finely chopped

COMBINE your pie filling, walnut flavoring, and walnuts with your Basic recipe.

PLACE mixture in your machine and follow manufacturer's directions in freezing.

MAKES
1 quart

Grape

Grape

Have you ever had grape ice cream? If you haven't tried it yet, be sure to make the plans and put the ingredients on your grocery list. A. S. A. P.

1 Basic recipe of your choice (p. 2–5)

1½ cups grape juice (I personally like the unsweetened grape juice)

1 lemon, juiced and zested

2–4 drops purple or violet food coloring (optional)

COMBINE your Basic recipe, lemon zest, and grape juice, and whisk until smooth.

PLACE mixture in your machine and follow manufacturer's directions in freezing.

DURING the last 5 minutes of mixing, fold in the lemon juice.

MAKES
1 quart

Pink Lemonade

Perfect for a pink lemonade pie, or even homemade popsicles,
this ice cream is refreshing, with a sweet and sour taste.

1 Basic recipe of your choice (p. 2–5)
½ cup pink lemonade concentrate
1 tsp. lemon extract
1 lemon, zested and juiced

ADD the pink lemonade concentrate, lemon extract, and zest to your Basic recipe, whisking together until combined.

PLACE mixture in your machine and follow manufacturer's directions in freezing.

DURING The last 5 minutes of the freezing process, add the lemon juice.

MAKES
1 quart

The Sweetness of Chocolate

Cookie Dough

Cookie Dough

I love to eat cookie dough right out of the mixer. Why would I not love chocolate chip cookie dough in a rich vanilla ice cream? I LOVE it.

1 Basic recipe of your choice (p. 2–5)
1 recipe Chocolate Chip Cookie Dough (below)

PLACE Basic recipe in your machine and follow manufacturer's directions in freezing.

PREPARE your cookie dough, and freeze dough in small teaspoons—the colder the better.

DURING the last 5 minutes of mixing, fold in small teaspoons of your frozen cookie dough.

CHOCOLATE CHIP COOKIE DOUGH

4 Tbsp. brown sugar
2 Tbsp. butter, soft
½ tsp. vanilla extract
2 Tbsp. milk
½ cup flour
½ cup mini semisweet chocolate chips

CREAM together the sugar and butter, add vanilla and milk.

FOLD in flour and stir until combined.

ADD chocolate chips.

DIVIDE dough into small teaspoon–size pieces and freeze.

ADD to ice cream according to recipe directions.

MAKES
1 quart

Cookies and Cream

Cookies and Cream

*Cookie and Cream has become a favorite ice cream flavor among the kids at my house.
Could even be the most requested flavor of ice cream out of this whole book.*

1 Basic recipe of your choice (p. 2–5)
3 cups crushed chocolate sandwich cookies

PLACE your Basic recipe in your machine and follow

manufacturer's directions in freezing.

DURING the last 5 minutes of mixing, fold in crushed cookies.

MAKES
1 quart

Still a Rocky Road

I prefer almonds in my rocky road ice cream, as well as a lot of marshmallows.

1 Basic recipe of your choice (p. 2–5)

⅓ cup cocoa

½ cup semisweet chocolate chips

½ cup roasted sliced almonds

2½ cups mini marshmallows

PLACE your Basic recipe, cocoa, and chocolate chips in a sauce pan.

WHISK together on medium heat until chocolate is smooth and no lumps appear.

REMOVE from the heat and cool completely in the fridge.

ADD cooled mixture in your machine and follow manufacturer's directions in freezing..

DURING the last 5 minutes of mixing, fold in almonds and marshmallows.

MAKES
1 quart

Mint Truffle

Mint and chocolate make a great pair, especially when you have a surprise,
like a mint truffle to complement your creamy ice cream.

1 Basic recipe of your choice (p. 2–5)

⅓ cup cocoa

½ cup semisweet chocolate chips

2 cups mint chocolate truffles, chopped and frozen

PLACE your Basic recipe, cocoa, and chocolate chips in a pan.

WHISK together on medium heat until chocolate is smooth and no lumps appear.

REMOVE from the heat and cool completely in the fridge.

PLACE your creamy mixture in your machine and follow manufacturer's directions in freezing.

DURING the last 5 minutes of mixing, fold in frozen mint chocolate truffles.

MAKES
1 quart

Mint Chocolate Chip

Mint Chocolate Chip

This is another child and adult favorite recipe. This quart of ice cream disappeared so fast!

1 Basic recipe of your choice (p. 2–5)

3–5 drops green food coloring

1 tsp. mint extract

2 cups mini chocolate chips (I prefer semisweet)

WHISK together your Basic recipe with green food coloring and mint extract.

PLACE your Basic mixture in your machine and follow manufacturer's directions in freezing.

DURING the last 5 minutes of mixing, fold in mini chocolate chips.

MAKES
1 quart

Chocolate
Raspberry Trifle

Chocolate Raspberry Trifle

This recipe is unlike any other chocolate ice cream recipe in this book.
It's super creamy and smooth, with a mousse-like consistency.

1 Basic recipe of your choice (p. 2–5)

1 (4 oz.) package chocolate pudding mix

1 recipe Fudge Brownies (p. 44)

2 cups fresh or frozen raspberries

WHISK together your Basic recipe with chocolate pudding mix.

PLACE your creamy mixture in your machine and follow manufacturer's directions in freezing.

DURING the last 5 minutes, add your brownie pieces and raspberries.

MAKES
1 quart

Silky Fudge

Silky Fudge

Honestly, this recipe should really be called "Death by Chocolate."

1 Basic recipe of your choice (p. 2–5)

⅓ cup cocoa

½ cup semisweet chocolate chips

1 recipe Chocolate Ganache (p. 88)

PLACE your Basic recipe, cocoa, and chocolate chips in a pan.

WHISK together on medium heat until chocolate is smooth and no lumps appear.

REMOVE from the heat and cool completely in the fridge.

PLACE your creamy mixture in your machine and follow manufacturer's directions in freezing.

DURING the last 5 minutes of mixing, fold in room-temperature Chocolate Ganache.

MAKES
1 quart

Chunky Brownie

Chunky Brownie

This recipe is all about what's on the inside that counts. And it doesn't get much better than chewy brownies in this silky chocolate ice cream.

1 Basic recipe of your choice (p. 2–5)
⅓ cup cocoa
½ cup semisweet chocolate chips
1 recipe Fudge Brownies (recipe on the following page, p. 44)

PLACE your Basic recipe, cocoa, and chocolate chips in a pan. Whisk together on medium heat until chocolate is smooth and no lumps appear.

REMOVE from heat and cool completely in fridge.

BAKE your brownies and cool. Cut into small chunks and freeze, by placing a single layer on a cookie sheet until cold.

PLACE your creamy mixture in your machine and follow manufacturer's directions in freezing.

DURING the last 5 minutes of mixing, fold in cold brownie chunks.

MAKES
1 quart

Fudge Brownies

½ cup butter

1 (12 oz.) bag dark chocolate, or semisweet chips

1 cup brown sugar

3 eggs

1¼ cups flour

pinch of salt

IN a large sauce pan, melt butter and dark chocolate chips on low, stirring frequently. Once melted, remove from heat and stir in sugar until well combined.

ADD eggs, one at a time, stirring in between. Add salt and flour, and mix until no flour is seen. Pour into a greased and cocoa-dusted 9 x 13 baking dish.

BAKE at 350 degrees for 25–28 minutes until middle is set, but not overdone.

COOL completely, and then break into small chunks.

SERVES
12–16

Burnt Almond Fudge

1 Basic recipe of your choice (p. 2–5)

⅓ cup cocoa

½ cup semisweet chocolate chips

1 tsp. almond extract

1 cup toasted almond slices

PLACE your Basic recipe, cocoa, chocolate chips, and almond extract in a sauce pan.

WHISK together on medium heat until chocolate is smooth and no lumps appear.

REMOVE from the heat and cool completely in the fridge.

PLACE your creamy mixture in your machine and follow manufacturer's directions in freezing. During the last 5 minutes, add your roasted almonds.

MAKES
1 quart

S'more Please?

S'more Please?

1 Basic recipe of your choice (p. 2–5)

⅓ cup cocoa

½ cup semisweet chocolate chips

1 cup mini chocolate chips (semisweet is best)

2 cups mini marshmallows

1 cup crushed graham crackers

PLACE your Basic recipe, cocoa, and chocolate chips in a sauce pan.

WHISK together on medium heat until chocolate is smooth and no lumps appear.

REMOVE from the heat and cool completely in the fridge.

PLACE your creamy mixture in your machine and follow manufacturer's directions in freezing.

DURING the last 5 minutes of mixing, add your mini chocolate chips,
marshmallows, and graham crackers.

MAKES
1 quart

Chocolate Toffee Crunch

*After making some great Chocolate Toffee Cake Bites, of course
I had to add this flavor to a chocolate ice cream.*

1 Basic recipe of your choice (p. 2–5)

⅓ cup cocoa

½ cup semisweet chocolate chips

2 crushed toffee pieces

PLACE your Basic recipe, cocoa, and chocolate chips in a saucepan.

WHISK together on medium heat until chocolate is smooth and
no lumps appear.

REMOVE from the heat and cool completely in the fridge.

PLACE your creamy mixture in your machine and follow
manufacturer's directions in freezing.

MAKES
1 quart

ADD your crushed toffee pieces during the last 5 minutes.

Chocolate Cinnamon

The flavors of cinnamon and chocolate are tickle-your-taste-buds good.

1 Basic recipe of your choice (p. 2–5)

⅓ cup cocoa

½ cup semisweet chocolate chips

1 Tbsp. cinnamon

PLACE your Basic recipe, cocoa, chocolate chips, and cinnamon in a sauce pan.

WHISK together on medium heat until chocolate is smooth and no lumps appear.

REMOVE from the heat and cool completely in the fridge.

PLACE your creamy mixture in your machine and follow manufacturer's directions in freezing.

MAKES
1 quart

Cherry
Chocolate

Cherry Chocolate

Juicy sweet cherries in rich and creamy ice cream, with Chocolate Ganache. Super fantastic!

1 Basic recipe of your choice (p. 2–5)
3 cups sweet cherries, pitted and halved
4 Tbsp. sugar
1 cup Chocolate Ganache (p. 88)

TOSS your cherries in sugar and roast in the oven at 300 degrees for 30 minutes.

REMOVE from the oven and cool covered until chilled.

CHOP into smaller pieces and add the cherries and juices to your Basic recipe.

PLACE mixture in your machine and follow manufacturer's directions in freezing.

DURING the last 5 minutes of mixing, fold in Chocolate Ganache.

MAKES
1 quart

Chocolate Hazelnut Truffle

I knew this idea for ice cream would be delicious.
Little did I know how fast it would disappear.

1 Basic recipe of your choice (p. 2–5)
1 ½ cups hazelnut spread
2 cups hazelnut truffles, diced

PLACE your Basic recipe and hazelnut spread in a medium saucepan.

WHISK together on medium heat until your hazelnut spread is smooth and no lumps appear.

REMOVE from the heat and cool completely in the fridge.

DICE your hazelnut truffles and place in the freezer to chill.

MAKES
1 quart

PLACE your hazelnut mixture in your machine and follow manufacturer's directions in freezing.

DURING the last 5 minutes of mixing, fold in cold hazelnut truffles.

Peanut Butter Chocolate Ripple

If you are a peanut butter lover like me, then you will love this recipe. It's smooth and creamy. Sinfully delicious.

1 Basic recipe of your choice (p. 2–5)
1 ½ cup creamy peanut butter
1 recipe Chocolate Ganache (p. 88)

IN a medium sauce pan, heat together your Basic recipe with the peanut butter until combined.

REMOVE from the heat and chill in the fridge.

PLACE your chilled creamy mixture in your machine and follow manufacturer's directions in freezing.

DURING the last 5 minutes of mixing, fold in the cold Chocolate Ganache

MAKES
1 quart

Holiday Treats

Brown Sugar

Brown Sugar

Using dark brown sugar is key to this recipe. This recipe would be delicious with pie or cobbler.

1 Basic recipe of your choice (p. 2–5), substituting dark brown sugar for the white sugar; same amount

WHISK together the dark brown sugar with the Basic recipe you choose.

PLACE your creamy mixture in your ice cream machine and follow manufacturer's directions in freezing.

MAKES
1 quart

The Cupcake

The Cupcake

I scream, you scream. We all scream for ice cream! What if it tasted like cake, or better yet, cupcakes? I couldn't pass up a cupcake-flavored ice cream—since I am Mrs. Cupcake.

1 Basic recipe of your choice (p. 2–5)
¾ cup yellow cake mix
½ cup rainbow sprinkles

WHISK together your Basic recipe and cake mix.

ADD mixture in your ice cream machine and follow manufacturer's directions in freezing.

FOLD in your rainbow sprinkles during the last 5 minutes.

MAKES
1 quart

Pepperminty

The holidays aren't complete without a scoop of peppermint ice cream on top of warm Fudge Brownies (p. 44), and a drizzle of Chocolate Fudge (p. 82). Happy Holidays!

1 Basic recipe of your choice (p. 2–5)

1½ cups peppermint chips or peppermint candies, crushed

2–3 drops of red food coloring

ADD your Basic recipe, peppermint chocolate mints or peppermint candies, and food coloring to your mixture in your ice cream machine and follow manufacturer's directions in freezing.

MAKES
1 quart

Root Beer Float

This recipe is for my son, who has become a lover of root beer flavored candy, cookies, cupcakes, and cake bites! This ice cream is delicious.

1 Basic recipe of your choice (p. 2–5)
2 Tbsp. Root Beer flavoring

WHISK your root beer flavoring with your Basic recipe.

ADD mixture to your ice cream machine and follow manufacturer's directions in freezing.

MAKES
1 quart

Cinnamon Bun

Cinnamon Bun

I am simply speechless . . . after eating this ice cream. It's a must-try.

1 Basic recipe of your choice (p. 2–5)

1 pkg. refrigerated cinnamon rolls

1 cup caramel sauce (I love Mrs. Richardson's)

2 Tbsp. cinnamon

½ cup chopped pecans (optional)

DICE your uncooked cinnamon rolls into small chunks. Spread evenly on a lightly greased cookie sheet.

BAKE at 350 degrees for 5–6 minutes.

REMOVE from the oven and toss, adding pecans (optional) and 1 tablespoon cinnamon. Return to the oven and bake another 5 minutes.

REMOVE from the oven and drizzle with packaged frosting and caramel sauce.

PLACE in the fridge to cool. Add Basic mixture and 1 tablespoon cinnamon to your ice cream machine and follow manufacturer's directions in freezing.

FOLD in your cinnamon caramel bites during the last 5 minutes of mixing.

MAKES
1 quart

Ginger Pumpkin
Spice

Ginger Pumpkin Spice

This recipe got 5 stars from all the taste testers. It's great—a perfect blend of spices and pumpkin.

1 Basic recipe of your choice (p. 2–5)

1½ cups pumpkin puree

1 tsp. ground ginger

1 tsp. cinnamon

1 tsp. cloves

1 tsp. allspice

WHISK together the spices and pumpkin puree with your Basic recipe.

ADD mixture in your ice cream machine and follow manufacturer's directions in freezing.

MAKES
1 quart

Egg Nog

Egg Nog

When Egg Nog appears in the grocery store, I know the holidays are just around the corner. Three cheers for Egg Nog!

1 Basic recipe of your choice (p. 2–5)

1 tsp. nutmeg

1 tsp. cinnamon

1 ½ tsp. rum extract or 2 tsp. dark rum

WHISK together the rum extract and spices with your Basic recipe.

ADD mixture in your ice cream machine and follow manufacturer's directions in freezing.

MAKES
1 quart

Dulce de Leche

This ice cream is a party in your mouth. Can you imagine what this caramel ice cream would taste like on top of apple pie? Even a chocolate cake would tickle your taste buds good.

1 Basic recipe of your choice (p. 2–5)
2 cups Dulce de Leche (boiled sweetened condensed milk)

WHISK together Basic recipe and Dulce de Leche until smooth.

ADD mixture in your ice cream machine and follow manufacturer's directions in freezing.

MAKES
1 quart

Fried Ice Cream

I know that I have mentioned in previous books about my love for churros. I especially love how they taste in this rich cinnamon ice cream. Most grocery stores now carry them in the freezer section—I've been known to bring home a box from a Costco book signing. I hide the box of churros behind the frozen chicken breasts. Brilliant, isn't it? Please, don't tell anyone. It will be our little secret.

1 Basic recipe of your choice (p. 2–5)

3 cups cooked and roughly chopped churros, chilled

1 tsp. cinnamon

PLACE your Basic recipe mixture and cinnamon in your machine and follow manufacturer's directions in freezing.

DURING the last 5 minutes of mixing, fold in your chopped, chilled churros.

MAKES
1 quart

Maple Bacon

Maple Bacon

Surprise! All I can say about this recipe is that if you like the salty and sweet flavors, or if you like anything with bacon—you'll fall in love with this recipe. Hint: use bacon that has been trimmed of fat. The crunchier the bacon, the better.

1 Basic recipe of your choice (p. 2–5)

2–3 tsp. maple flavoring

1 lb. bacon, trimmed of the fat, cooked, cooled, and crumbled

COMBINE your maple flavoring and cooked and cooled bacon.

ADD mixture in your ice cream machine and follow manufacturer's directions in freezing.

MAKES
1 quart

Peanut Butter Bliss

Peanut Butter Bliss

A peanut butter overload—but in a more positive light, it should be Peanut Butter Bliss.

1 Basic recipe of your choice (p. 2–5)

3 cups creamy peanut butter

1 cup peanut butter cups, chopped and frozen

IN a medium sauce pan, heat together 1½ cups peanut butter with your Basic recipe, until combined. Remove from the heat and chill in the fridge.

PLACE your chilled creamy mixture in your machine and follow manufacturer's directions in freezing.

DURING the last 5 minutes of mixing, fold in peanut butter cups and 1½ cups creamy peanut butter.

MAKES
1 quart

Pralines and Cream

Silky caramel and crunchy pecans make this ice cream fabulous!

1 Basic recipe of your choice (p. 2–5)
1 cup toasted chopped pecans
1 cup caramel sauce (I am a huge fan of Mrs. Richardson's)

PLACE your Basic recipe mixture in your machine and follow manufacturer's directions in freezing.

DURING the last 5 minutes of mixing, fold in your chopped pecans and caramel sauce.

MAKES
1 quart

Boston Cream Pie

*I love the flavors of custard and chocolate sauce. This ice cream is a hit—
especially when paired with a warm, rich chocolate cake.*

1 Basic recipe of your choice (I recommend Rich and Creamy Vanilla, p. 2)

2 egg yolks

1 recipe Chocolate Ganache (p. 88)

COMBINE your Basic recipe and egg yolks in a medium sauce pan.

COOK until thickened, about 10 minutes over medium heat, stirring constantly.

REMOVE custard from the heat and chill.

PLACE mixture in your machine and follow manufacturer's directions in freezing.

DURING the last 5 minutes of mixing, fold in your Chocolate Ganache,
leaving large pieces and ribbons of chocolate throughout the ice cream.

MAKES
1 quart

Hot Chocolate Chili

Hot Chocolate Chili

1 Basic recipe of your choice (p. 2–5)

⅓ cup cocoa

½ cup semisweet chocolate chips

1 Tbsp. cinnamon

1 Tbsp. chili powder

PLACE your Basic recipe, cocoa, chocolate chips, and spices in a medium saucepan.

WHISK together on medium heat until chocolate is smooth and no lumps appear.

REMOVE from heat and cool completely in fridge.

PLACE creamy mixture in your machine and follow manufacturer's directions in freezing.

MAKES
1 quart

Serendipity

Serendipity

What do you call a surprisingly good ice cream? An ice cream that shocked every single person who tasted it? I call it pure genius—well, maybe that's a little much. My husband did have serious doubts about my level of craziness until he ate his first spoonful. You see, one bite is not enough. (Hint: This recipe would be excellent served with an apple crisp, peach cobbler, or any berry pie.)

1 Basic recipe of your choice (p. 2–5)
3 sweet corn cobs, husked and rinsed (fresh is best)
1 tsp. vanilla

CUT all your corn off the cob and then cut your corn cobs in half.

STEEP the corn and cobs in your Basic recipe in a large saucepan, and cook over medium heat for 30 minutes, stirring frequently. Add vanilla.

REMOVE from the heat and strain your custard. Refrigerate until chilled.

PLACE your custard mixture in your machine and follow manufacturer's directions in freezing.

MAKES
1 quart

The Alice (Black Licorice)

In honor of those of you who asked for a black licorice ice cream (Alan), this one is for you.
This is also for the great little store called The Hummingbird in Arlee, Montana, that has over 55 kinds of licorice, mostly black.

1 Basic recipe of your choice (p. 2–5)

2 tsp. anise extract

PLACE your Basic recipe mixture and flavoring in your machine and follow manufacturer's directions in freezing.

MAKES
1 quart

Topping it All Off

Chocolate Fudge

You can't go wrong with serving this fudge sauce over your ice cream—any ice cream, really. Chocolate makes most good food great.

1 (14 oz.) can sweetened condensed milk (you can use the fat-free version)

2 tsp. vanilla extract

¾ cup semisweet chocolate chips

¼ cup whole cream

WHISK together all ingredients over medium heat in a sauce pan until chocolate is melted. Serve warm over ice cream.

GREAT for the Ultimate Banana Split (p. 111), or The Sundae (p. 113).

MAKES
2 Cups

Peanut Butter Silk

I've always been a fan of peanut butter. Peanut butter on pancakes, peanut butter on ice cream, peanut butter on celery . . . It's how I get my kids to eat their veggies when they are in a stubborn mood. Which is more often than I would like.

1 cup sugar

½ cup water

1 cup peanut butter

OVER MEDIUM HEAT, Simmer sugar and water together until sugar is dissolved—approximately 5 minutes.

ONCE your sugar is dissolved, add your peanut butter and whisk together until smooth.

SERVE warm over your ice cream, sliced bananas, or chocolate cake . . . The sky is the limit—let your imagination go wild!

MAKES
2 Cups

Magical Shell

Cracking the chocolate shell is sometimes the best about eating ice cream and chocolate sauce. This two-ingredient recipe is simple and usually I have them stocked in my fridge or freezer at all times. Let's face it—if I could eat only two things the rest of my life (and not gain weight or have health problems), butter and chocolate would most likely be on the list.

1 cup semisweet chocolate chips
¼ cup butter

GENTLY melt chocolate chips and butter together until smooth.

SERVE over ice cream. Sauce will harden as it cools.

MAKES
1 Cup

Creamy Caramel

How can you go wrong with a sauce as beautiful as this? Caramel can be intimidating, but once you try it, you will be hooked. Think of how good a homemade caramel sauce would be over the top of a warm apple pie? Really, that good.

1 1/2 cup brown sugar
1/2 cup butter
3/4 cup heavy cream
1 tsp. vanilla

POUR sugar and butter into a small sauce pan.

HEAT over medium until sugar mixture bubbles, cooking 5–8 minutes.

REMOVE from heat and add ¾ cup heavy cream and 1 teaspoon vanilla.

SERVE while warm. If your caramel cools, reheat in the microwave for 30 seconds at a time, stirring in between. (If you are worried about your caramel hardening, add 2 Tbsp. light corn syrup before removing from the heat.)

MAKES
1½ Cups

Whipped Cream

My kids don't like whipped cream. I often wonder where they came from.
I eat it from the spoon . . . and I even lick the beater sometimes.
There. I feel much better now after sharing that with you.

2 cups heavy whipping cream

¼–½ cup powdered sugar (depending on preference)

POUR cream into a large mixing bowl and mix at low speed.

GRADUALLY increase speed until the mixer is on high. Watch for cream to become thicker and soft peaks form.

TURN off the mixer and add the sugar. Start slowly again—no messes today!

BEAT until stiff peaks form. Remember there is a fine line between butter and whipped cream. Now is not the time to change the laundry or check your email.

MAKES
2½ Cups

Raspberry Glaze

One summer, our neighbors told me I could have as many of their raspberries as I could pick. I was there every day for months on end, picking and eating my fair share of raspberries. Most of the time the bowl was eaten before we got home, but on rare occasions, we were able to make some raspberry glaze for the Ann's Lemon Supreme recipe (p. 9). It was heavenly, to say the least.

2 cups fresh or frozen raspberries

4 Tbsp. sugar

2 Tbsp. cornstarch

2 Tbsp. water

2 tsp. raspberry extract

SMASH raspberries through a strainer and squeeze the berries until all the juices come clean.

TRANSFER the juices to a medium saucepan and add sugar, cornstarch, and water. Simmer for 5–10 minutes until thickened.

ADD raspberry extract and stir to combine. Serve over ice cream, cheesecake, or pancakes and waffles.

MAKES
2 Cups

Chocolate Ganache

Chocolate Ganache is my favorite go-to chocolate sauce recipe. While warm, it can glide over the top of a bunt cake, or if you chill it, it becomes thick and spreadable, like frosting.

1 cup heavy whipping cream

12 oz. semi-sweet chocolate chunks or chips

HEAT the cream in a saucepan until it comes to a boil.

REMOVE cream and pour over chocolate in a mixing bowl.

STIR to mix together until smooth.

MAKES
2½ **Cups**

Mint Chocolate Glaze

How about a chocolate sauce with minty flavor? That's what I was thinking too. I really can't say enough about this sauce. It's so gooooooooooood.

¾ cup light corn syrup

½ cup semisweet chocolate chips

1 tsp. mint extract

HEAT all ingredients over medium heat until chocolate is melted and combined, making a smooth glaze. Serve warm.

MAKES
1 Cup

Maple Cream

This sauce would be perfect paired with the Maple Bacon ice cream (p. 71) or the Ginger Pumpkin Spice ice cream (p. 65), or even paired with the any Basic recipe and the Cinnamon Roasted Mixed Nuts (p. 92)

1 cup heavy cream

1 Tbsp. maple flavoring

2 Tbsp. pure maple syrup

WHISK all ingredients together and simmer for 5 minutes, stirring occasionally.

REMOVE from the heat and serve warm.

MAKES
1 Cup

Blueberry Sauce

For this sauce, I prefer whole blueberries so I kept it that way. If you prefer a smooth sauce, you can strain the berries just before serving. Either way, it's a great sauce to serve over any dessert, from ice cream to cheesecake. Two of my favorite treats.

2 cups blueberries, fresh or frozen

½ cup sugar

1 tsp. lemon juice

½ tsp. cinnamon

1 tsp. cornstarch

SIMMER together berries, sugar, lemon juice, cinnamon, and cornstarch over medium heat for 5–8 minutes.

REMOVE from heat and serve warm.

MAKES
2½ Cups

Cinnamon Roasted Mixed Nuts

These nuts are good alone, and even better when served over the top of ice cream with Chocolate Fudge (p. 82), or Maple Cream (p. 90)

1 cup sugar

⅓ cup water

1 tsp. nutmeg

1 tsp. cinnamon

1 tsp. cloves

½ tsp. salt

1 cup each pecans, peanuts, and almonds, roughly chopped

PLACE the nuts on a large baking sheet in a single layer. Bake at 350 degrees for 12 minutes and remove. Meanwhile, mix together sugar, water, and spices in a saucepan.

MAKES
3 Cups

COOK over medium heat for 8–10 minutes. Add your roasted mixed nuts into your saucepan, stirring to combine. Mix until nuts are coated evenly.

SPREAD nuts on a parchment-lined baking sheet until cool. Break apart with your fork, unless you want them clumped together.

STORE in an airtight container for up to 1 week, at room temperature.

Milkshake Perfection

Triple Chocolate

Or death by chocolate—it's a great milkshake. For the chocolate lovers.

4 cups Silky Fudge ice cream (p. 41)

1½–2 cups milk (whole or 2% is best)

1 cup Chocolate Fudge (p. 82)

BLEND all ingredients together until smooth.

SERVES
4

Chocolate Peanut Butter Cookie Dough

Holy cow. What a perfect combination of flavors—all of my favorite things are in this recipe.

2 cups Cookie Dough ice cream (p. 31)

2 cups Silky Fudge ice cream (p. 41)

½ cup creamy peanut butter

1½–2 cups milk (whole or 2% is best)

BLEND all ingredients together until smooth.

SERVES
4

Cookies and
Cream

Cookies and Cream

For my Ethan. This is your milkshake creation. I love you!

4 cups Cookies and Cream ice cream (p. 33)
10 chocolate sandwich cookies
1½–2 cups milk (whole or 2% is best)

BLEND all ingredients together until smooth.

TOP with Chocolate Fudge (p. 82) and Whipped Cream (p. 86)

USE a thick straw for this shake. I guarantee you'll need it!

SERVES
4

Peanut Butter Cup

Yummy to my tummy. I am hungry for this milkshake now, as I type this recipe.
Good thing I have some ice cream in my freezer, right?

4 cups Peanut Butter Bliss ice cream (p. 73)
6 unwrapped peanut butter cups
1½–2 cups milk (whole or 2% is best)

BLEND all ingredients together until smooth.

SERVES
4

White Chocolate Roasted Strawberry

I think that there are certain things in life worth celebrating.
This milkshake is certainly one of those good things.

4 cups Roasted Strawberry ice cream (p. 11)

1 cup fresh strawberries, washed and hulled

½ cup melted white chocolate

1½–2 cups milk (whole or 2% is best)

BLEND all ingredients together until smooth.

SERVES
4

Frozen Mexican
Hot Chocolate

Frozen Mexican Hot Chocolate

How about a cold glass of Mexican Hot Chocolate on a warm summers' evening?

4 cups Hot Chocolate Chili ice cream (p. 77)

1½–2 cups milk (whole or 2% is best)

dash of cinnamon

BLEND all ingredients together until smooth.

TOP with Whipped Cream. (p. 86)

SERVES
4

Magnificent Mint

Let's face the truth. I could have done an entire book about milkshakes. Yes, that's right.
101 milkshakes . . . But since I didn't, this recipe had to make this book.

4 cups Mint Truffle (p. 35) or Mint Chocolate Chip ice cream (p. 37)

½ cup Chocolate Fudge (p. 82)

1½–2 cups milk (whole or 2% is best)

BLEND all ingredients together until smooth.

SERVES
4

Going Bananas

On the advice of my husband, this recipe had to be included.
What's better than bananas, chocolate, and peanut butter?

4 cups Hunky Monkey ice cream (p. 15)

1 cup cream peanut butter

1½–2 cups milk (whole or 2 % is best)

BLEND all ingredients together until smooth.

SERVES
4

Lemon
Raspberry

Lemon Raspberry

Did I say how refreshing Ann's Lemon Supreme ice cream is? Well, if I didn't let me say it here.
Put it together with the Raspberry glaze and you've got yourself an amazing milkshake.

4 cups Ann's Lemon Supreme ice cream (p. 9)

1 cup Raspberry Glaze (p. 87)

1 cup fresh raspberries

1½–2 cups milk (whole or 2% is best)

BLEND all ingredients together until smooth.

SERVES
4

Lemon Coconut

*I'm happy just imagining this in a tall, cold glass, with a thick straw . . .
in the middle of the pool (or ocean), basking in the sun.*

2 cups Cancún Coconut Basic recipe (p. 5)

2 cups Ann's Lemon Supreme (p. 9)

1½–2 cups milk (whole or 2% is best)

BLEND all ingredients together until smooth.

SERVES
4

Pumpkin Pie

Need I say more? Really, it's pretty darn tasty.

4 cups Ginger Pumpkin Spice ice cream (p. 65)

1 cup gingersnap cookies, crushed

1½–2 cups milk (whole or 2% is best)

BLEND all ingredients together until smooth.

SERVES
4

Ice Cream Treats

Ultimate
Banana Split

Ultimate Banana Split

Ever wonder how to make the best banana split around? Like the one you get at an ice cream shop?
There's no need to go out anymore. You can make one in your own kitchen.

1 banana, peeled and separated lengthwise

1 scoop Roasted Strawberry ice cream (p. 11)

1 scoop Silky Fudge ice cream (p. 41)

1 scoop Mint Chocolate Chip ice cream (p. 37)

½ cup Chocolate Fudge (p. 82)

½ cup Creamy Caramel (p. 85)

½ cup Magical Shell (p. 84)

Whipped Cream (p. 86)

maraschino Cherries (optional, but necessary in my book)

Cinnamon Roasted Mixed Nuts (p. 92) (optional, but sometimes
   necessary depending on my mood)

PLACE banana in your bowl, and top in a row with ice cream scoops.

ON the Roasted Strawberry ice cream, place the Chocolate Fudge sauce.
On the Silky Fudge ice cream, place your Creamy Caramel sauce. And finally,
for your Mint Chocolate Chip ice cream, top with the Magical Shell.

FREELY cover the ice creams with the nuts (optional), Whipped Cream,
and last, but not least, the maraschino cherries.

SERVES 1 very hungry person or 3–4 moderately hungry people.

SERVES
1–4

The Sundae

The Sundae

For this recipe, the larger the bowl, the better The Sundae is. It's also fun to make a family serving, and then serve from the bowl to individual bowls, or you can all have your own spoon.

4 brownie pieces, cut into 2 ☐ squares

3 scoops of ice cream (You have plenty of options to choose from: my favorites would be, well, any recipe from The Sweetness of Chocolate section.)

Whipped Cream (p. 86)

Chocolate Fudge (p. 82)

Cinnamon Roasted Mixed Nuts (p. 92)

Creamy Caramel (p. 85)

LAYER your brownies and then ice cream. Then the Chocolate Fudge, the Whipped Cream and Spicy Nuts, and then the Creamy Caramel.

YUM . . .

HELPFUL HINT: warm the brownies and the Fudge Sauce.

SERVES
1-4

Ice Cream
Sandwich

Ice Cream Sandwich

*With the ice cream sandwich, most good cookies could easily make the base for this recipe.
How to choose? Well, if you need some more ideas, be sure to check out my cookie book,*
101 Gourmet Cookies *(shameless plug). I would try the Spectacular Snickerdoodle,
the Browned Butter Crinkle, the Whoopie Pie, and the list could go on and on . . .
but the recipe I am going to share with you is our family favorite.*

ice cream—your favorite recipe (from this book, right?), softened

1 recipe Chocolate Chip Pudding cookies (recipe on the following page, p. 116)

sprinkles

nuts, chopped

candies, crushed

chocolate chips

PLACE a small scoop of ice cream in the center of your cookie, taking the second cookie
and gently pressing together until the ice cream comes evenly to the sides.

ROLL your cookie in any goodies you desire, then place again in the freezer
until set, about 20 minutes.

STORE in an airtight container.

MAKES
15–18

Chocolate Chip Pudding Cookies

from *101 Gourmet Cookies for Everyone*

1 cup butter, softened

¼ cup sugar

¾ cup brown sugar

1 tsp. vanilla

2 eggs

1 (4 oz.) pkg. vanilla instant pudding mix—powder only

1 tsp. baking soda

2¼ cups flour

2 cups semisweet chocolate chips

CREAM together butter and sugars until light and fluffy. Add vanilla, eggs, and pudding mix (dry powder only).

IN a separate bowl, mix together baking soda and flour and gently add to wet ingredients. Fold in chocolate chips.

MAKES 30

USE a small cookie scoop to drop dough onto lightly greased cookie sheet.

BAKE at 350 degrees for 8–10 minutes, until sides become golden.

REMOVE from the oven and cool completely on a wire rack.

Bananas Foster

The summer I came up with this recipe, it was a hit among my neighbors . . .
this is a great dessert to share after a wonderful party or BBQ.

1 stick butter

2 cups light brown sugar

1 tsp. vanilla

½ tsp. imitation rum extract

½ tsp. ground nutmeg

4–6 bananas, ripe

ice cream—I would recommend the Dulce de Leche (p. 68),
   Rich and Creamy Vanilla (p. 2), Pralines and Cream (p. 74),
   or Fried Ice Cream (p. 69).

IN a heavy saucepan, melt butter, sugar, nutmeg, vanilla, and imitation rum extract.

BRING to a boil over medium heat and boil 1 minute.

SLICE bananas and spoon sauce over bananas and ice cream.

SERVES
6

Chocolate Cups

Chocolate Cups

So simple really. Perfect for an ice cream party, a birthday party, or even a wedding reception.
Great for use in an ice cream buffet. And, of course, a cupcake liner is used to streamline this project.
Yay for cupcake liners!

1 recipe Chocolate Ganache (p. 88), warm

24 cupcake liners

24 cupcake pans

cupcake pans

small spoon

PLACE your cupcake liners in your cupcake tins. Spray a small, I mean teeny-tiny amount, of cooking spray in each liner.

USING your spoon, place about 2 tablespoons of Chocolate Ganache into each cupcake liner, spreading around all sides and bottom of the liner, making sure not to miss anything.

PLACE the liners in the freezer or fridge to set up. Serve with your favorite ice cream.

MAKES
24

Chocolate-Dipped
Cones

Chocolate-Dipped Cones

So simple really. Perfect for an ice cream party, a birthday party, or even a wedding reception. Great for use in an ice cream buffet.

1 recipe Chocolate Ganache (p. 88), warm

18–24 medium ice cream cones

rainbow sprinkles

candies, crushed

nuts, chopped

TAKE a small ¼ cup scoop and place warm chocolate inside each cone, one at a time.

GENTLY roll cone around to allow chocolate to cover all sides, including a little on the outside top of the cone.

GENTLY dip the top outside edge of your cone into toppings, such as sprinkles, nuts, or crushed candies.

LET stand to set for 10 minutes.

FILL with your favorite ice creams and eat!

MAKES
18-24

Cookie Dough Cups

Cookie Dough Cups

Another great use for my favorite chocolate chip cookie recipe—I use these beautiful mini bundt pans. And the detailing is so pretty!

Chocolate Chip Pudding Cookies recipe (p. 116)
muffin pan

GENEROUSLY grease your muffin pan.

SHAPE your cookie dough as you would a pie crust around the inside of the muffin pan.

BAKE according to the recipe directions until cookies are light golden. The cookie will puff up slightly but shrink down as it cools. Remove the cups once they are cooled completely.

P. S. If you want, freeze some of the bowls for later use. Seal tight and label. The bowls will last for up to a month in an airtight container in the freezer.

MAKES
30–36

Ice Cream Fondue

Several flavors of ice cream, frozen on a stick. Warm, rich chocolate to dip your ice cream into . . . what a great party idea. Thanks, Holly—who said you couldn't put ice cream on a stick?

small scoops of ice cream

small sucker or popsicle sticks

fondue pot

Chocolate Fudge (p. 82)

FREEZE your ice cream scoops with a stick placed ¾ of the way through each scoop for at least 20 minutes until set.

PREPARE your fudge sauce and keep warm. Serve ice cream and fudge sauce, dipping each ice cream individually into the sauce.

SERVES endless amounts of people, depending on how many people you invite over.

SERVES
Everyone!

Ice Cream Cakes

Cookies and Cream

Cookies + Ice Cream + Chocolate Cake = Sinfully delicious cake

2 cups Rich and Creamy Vanilla ice cream (p. 2)

2 cups Cookies and Cream ice cream (p. 33)

1 box chocolate cake mix

3 eggs

1 tsp. vanilla extract

1 cup milk

1 recipe Whipped Cream (p. 86)

1 recipe Chocolate Fudge (p. 82)

12 whole chocolate sandwich cookies, cut in half

2 cups crushed chocolate sandwich cookies

MIX together the cake mix, eggs, vanilla, and milk.

POUR into 2 (9-inch) round baking pans, buttered and dusted with cocoa powder.

BAKE at 350 degrees for 20–25 minutes, until cake springs back when lightly touched. Remove from the oven and cool completely.

SERVES
10-12

PLACE in the freezer until ready to assemble. Slice each round in half.

SPREAD the ice cream, alternating the flavors, approximately 1½ cups ice cream each layer.

AFTER each layer is done, freeze until set, about 20 minutes. Then repeat until all the layers are done.

TOP with Whipped Cream and drizzle with Chocolate Fudge and sprinkle with crushed sandwich cookies for garnish. With the cookies cut in half, circle around the cake, flat side down.

Berry Angel

My sister suggested I make this beautiful dessert—it's something that her mother-in-law serves
for special occasions—and since they are ice cream lovers, I highly recommend trying
this recipe. It's really good.

1 angel food cake, cut into 4 sections, horizontally

2 cups Roasted Strawberry ice cream (p. 11), softened

2 cups Sour Cream Blueberry ice cream (p. 19), softened

2 cups Triple Berry ice cream (p. 16), softened

1 recipe Whipped Cream (p. 86)

I LIKE TO put this beautiful creation on a cake stand. Place your bottom layer of cake down, and top with your Roasted Strawberry ice cream, spreading evenly across the cake. Place your middle layer of cake on top and freeze for 20 minutes until set.

REMOVE from the freezer and layer your Sour Cream Blueberry ice cream, spreading evenly across the middle cake layer. Place in the freezer for 20 minutes until set.

LAST, remove from the freezer and layer your piece of cake on top and spread the Triple Berry ice cream, just like the other layers—placing the final piece of cake on top. Freeze again for 20 minutes.

FINALLY, you are ready to frost with the Whipped Cream. Take your frozen cake out, and frost with the whipping cream, being generous … you can't have too much, right? Well, within reason—and once you're done, place back into the freezer until ready to serve.

SERVES
6–8

Red Velvet

Red Velvet

This recipe is an adaptation of the traditional southern red velvet cake . . .
But I think you will find that it's a great "updated" way to serve.

1 recipe Rich and Creamy Vanilla (p. 2)
1 box red velvet cake mix
2 eggs
1 tsp. vanilla
1 cup sour cream
½ cup milk

MIX together the cake mix, eggs, vanilla extract, sour cream, and milk.

BAKE your cake in buttered and floured jelly roll pan, lined with parchment paper. Bake at 250 degrees for 20–25 minutes, until cake springs back when lightly touched.

REMOVE from the oven and cool completely. Gently loosen around the edges of the cake with a knife.

SPREAD your softened ice cream over the entire cake surface, leaving a 1-inch edge around the whole cake.

GENTLY, but quickly, start to roll your cake, loosening the parchment paper as you go, tucking the cake firmly. Some ice cream will come out of the ends, but most will remain inside the rolled cake.

PLACE back in the freezer for 30-45 minutes to set.

REMOVE from the freezer and slice into 1- or 2-inch slices to serve.

TOP with a serving of Whipped Cream (p. 86) if desired.

SERVES
10–12

Mint Brownie Explosion

This is chocolate and mint flavoring at it's finest. It's a beautiful way to serve your brownies and ice cream . . . Super simple and fun. You can't go wrong with that!

1 (9 x 13) pan of brownies, baked and cooled
½ recipe Mint Truffle ice cream (p. 35), softened
1 recipe Mint Chocolate Glaze (p. 89)
1 recipe Whipped Cream (p. 86)
chocolate shavings for garnish

SPREAD your softened ice cream over the top of your chilled brownie pan.

SPREAD evenly, taking care to reach all the edges. Place in the freezer for 20 minutes to set.

MEANWHILE, make your Whipped Cream. Remove your brownie pan from the freezer and drizzle with half of the Mint Chocolate Glaze and top with Whipped Cream.

DRIZZLE again with remaining glaze, and place in the freezer to set. Let stand at room temperature for 5 minutes before serving.

HELPFUL HINT: cutting this dessert is easier with a hot knife.

SERVES
12-15

Pepperminty Chocolate Cream

'Tis the season for great treats . . . and just because it's winter doesn't mean you can't enjoy an ice cream treat.

4 cups Pepperminty ice cream (p. 60), softened

1 box chocolate cake mix

3 eggs

1 tsp. vanilla extract

2 cups sour cream

Whipped Cream (p. 86)

Chocolate Fudge (p. 82)

candy canes, crushed

MIX together the cake mix, eggs, vanilla, and sour cream. Pour into 2 (9-inch) round baking pans, greased and dusted with cocoa powder.

BAKE at 350 degrees for 20–25 minutes, until cake springs back when lightly touched. Remove from the oven and cool completely.

PLACE in the freezer until ready to assemble. Slice each round in half, horizontally.

SPREAD the ice cream, 1 cup plus ¼ cup, for each layer, placing the cake round on top, then freeze until set, about 20 minutes. Then repeat until all the layers are done.

TOP with Whipped Cream, drizzle with Chocolate Fudge, and sprinkle with crushed candy canes for garnish.

SERVES
8–10

Chocolate Raspberry Trifle

Thank heavens for good treats. I think that I should end every day with a great dessert. Well, maybe not every day—but there is always a reason to bake.

3 cups Silky Fudge ice cream (p. 41), softened

3 cups Rich and Creamy Vanilla ice cream (p. 2), softened

Whipped Cream (p. 86)

fresh raspberries (about 2 cups)

1 box dark chocolate cake mix

3 eggs

1 cup milk

1 tsp. vanilla extract

½ cup softened butter

MIX together the cake mix, eggs, milk, vanilla, and softened butter until combined.

BAKE at 350 degrees for 20–25 minutes in a 9 x 13 baking pan until cake springs back when lightly touched. Remove from the oven and cool completely.

SERVES
12

CUT your cake into small 2-inch pieces. Layer your freezer proof bowl with chocolate cake, ¼ of the raspberries, Silky Fudge ice cream, then Rich and Creamy Vanilla ice cream.

PLACE in the freezer for 20 minutes until set. Then repeat until all cake, ice creams, and raspberries are used and bowl is full.

PLACE in the freezer until ready to serve. Top with Whipped Cream and more raspberries if desired.

Ice Cream Pies

Ultimate S'more

Ultimate S'more

S'more Please? Ice cream with a chocolate cookie crust, topped with
marshmallows and Chocolate Fudge . . . A little slice of heaven.

1 (9-inch) chocolate cookie or graham cracker crust

1 cup Chocolate Ganache (p. 88)

2½–3 cups Silky Fudge (p. 41), softened

10–12 medium scoops S'more Please? ice cream (p. 47)

2 cups mini chocolate candy bars, broken

1 cup mini marshmallows

½ cup crushed graham crackers

SPREAD your Chocolate Ganache over the bottom of your crust in an even layer.

TOP the ganache with a layer of your Silky Fudge ice cream. Place in freezer
for 20 minutes, until set.

PLACE scoops of the S'more Please? ice cream close together, filling the
entire surface of the pie.

COVER the top of your pie with the mini chocolate candy bars
and scatter with mini marshmallows.

SPRINKLE with crushed graham crackers.

KEEP pie in freezer until ready to serve.

SERVES
6–8

Grasshopper

*This is one of my favorite ice cream pies. Topped with whipped cream—
the taller this pie is, the better.*

1 (9-inch) chocolate cookie pie crust

1 cup Chocolate Ganache (p. 88)

4–5 cups Mint Truffle (p. 35) or Mint Chocolate Chip (p. 37) ice cream, softened

1 recipe Whipped Cream (p. 86)

chocolate shavings for garnish

SPREAD your ganache in an even layer in the pie crust.

TOP with your soft ice cream, spreading evenly. The taller the pie the better.
If you want, add another cup of ice cream.

SPREAD your whipped cream and garnish with the chocolate shavings.

FREEZE until set, 20–30 minutes or until ready to serve.

SERVES
6-8

Chocolate Peanut Butter

This pie is a beauty! It's almost too pretty to eat . . . I said almost. It's impressive to the eye, and also to your taste buds. Perfect treat to finish up that special dinner . . . it leaves your guests talking.

1 (9-inch) graham cracker or chocolate cookie crust

2½ cups Silky Fudge (p. 41), softened

1 cup Chocolate Ganache (p. 88)

2½ cups Peanut Butter Bliss (p. 73), softened

3 cups mini chocolate peanut butter cups, cut in half

1 recipe Peanut Butter Silk (p. 83)

1 recipe Whipped Cream (p. 86)

SPREAD your Silky Fudge ice cream over the bottom of your pie crust.

FREEZE for 20 minutes until set. Then layer the ganache and the Peanut Butter Bliss ice cream.

RETURN to the freezer for another 20 minutes. Line the outside of the pie with the cut peanut butter cups, and drizzle the entire pie with Peanut Butter Silk sauce.

TOP each piece with Whipped Cream when serving.

SERVES
6–8

Key Lime

Key Lime

I still have fond memories of eating my first Key Lime pie in Key West, Florida. This ice cream pie is a fantastic pair to the classic version.

1 (9-inch) graham cracker crust

4 cups Key Lime Pie ice cream (p. 13), softened

1 recipe Whipped Cream (p. 86)

grated lime zest, for garnish

½ cup crushed graham crackers

SPREAD your softened ice cream in the graham cracker crust evenly, making the center slightly higher than the sides.

TOP with whipped cream, lime zest, and graham crackers.

FREEZE for 20–30 minutes or until ready to serve.

SERVES
6–8

Muddy Mississippi

A southern favorite . . . I'm channeling my best southern accent and am prepared to knock your socks off with this great ice cream pie. Y'all have a great time eating it!

1 (9-inch) chocolate pie crust

4 cups Silky Fudge ice cream (p. 41), softened

2½ cups mini marshmallows

2 cups Chocolate Ganache (p. 88), warm

1 cup pecans or walnuts, chopped (I'm a pecan girl)

SMOOTH the ice cream into the bottom of the pie crust.

FREEZE your pie for 20 minutes to set. Then top your ice cream with the mini marshmallows.

MIX your chopped nuts with the warm chocolate ganache and spread over the top of the marshmallows.

RETURN to the freezer for 30 minutes until ready to serve.

SERVES
6-8

Chocolate Toffee Crunch

I have become obsessed with toffee—toffee cupcakes, toffee cake bites, and now toffee ice cream pies. This is an ultimate toffee-lovers recipe.

1 (9-inch) chocolate cookie crust

4 cups Chocolate Toffee Crunch (p. 48)

1 cup caramel sauce (I love Mrs. Richardson's, or my own Creamy Caramel recipe (p. 85)

1–1½ cups Chocolate Fudge (p. 82)

2 cups crushed toffee pieces

LAYER half of your ice cream in the chocolate cookie crust.

SPRINKLE half of your toffee pieces and top with remaining ice cream.

DRIZZLE with caramel sauce and fudge sauce and sprinkle with the remaining toffee pieces.

SERVES
6–8

Baked Alaska

Baked Alaska

I couldn't write an ice cream book and not include a Baked Alaska recipe. It's a gourmet dessert and can be enjoyed by everyone. You can make this recipe your own by mixing up the flavors of the ice cream inside.

1 9-inch pie shell, baked and cooled

Roasted Strawberry ice cream (p. 11)

5 egg whites

½ cup sugar

½ tsp. cream of tartar

PREPARE your pie shell by baking and cooling according to package directions.

PLACE your softened ice cream in the center of the pie shell, smoothing out carefully to the edges, mounding ice cream, the center higher than the sides.

FREEZE until solid—approximately 20 minutes.

WHISK together your egg whites and cream of tartar until stiff peaks form. Whisking by hand is better and recommended for the meringue preparation. Slowly add your sugar.

SPREAD your egg meringue on top of your ice cream and place in a 500 degree oven for 2–3 minutes.

WATCH carefully and remove when golden. Serve immediately.

SERVES
6–8

Recipe Index

About the Author

WENDY L. PAUL has been cooking and baking for many years. She enjoys writing new recipes and creating easy-to-make dinners and desserts. Her baking skills have been featured on numerous morning TV shows and news programs. When Wendy is working on a project—whether home improvement, a new recipe, or shopping at a craft store—she is truly happy. She is the bestselling author of *101 Gourmet Cupcakes in 10 Minutes*, *101 Gourmet Cookies for Everyone*, and *101 Gourmet Cake Bites for All Occasions*. She and her family live in Utah, and oddly enough, have a dog named Cupcake. For more information, visit her website at www.wendypaulcreations.com.

About *the* Photographer

MARIELLE HAYES is a photographer based in the San Francisco Bay Area. She loves her family, seasonal candy, high heels, art museums, sequins, bargain hunting, traveling, action movies, and being behind the camera.